OAKLAND
RAIDERS

BY PATRICK KELLEY

SportsZone

An Imprint of Abdo Publishing
abdopublishing.com

abdopublishing.com

Published by Abdo Publishing, a division of ABDO, PO Box 398166, Minneapolis, Minnesota 55439. Copyright © 2017 by Abdo Consulting Group, Inc. International copyrights reserved in all countries. No part of this book may be reproduced in any form without written permission from the publisher. SportsZone™ is a trademark and logo of Abdo Publishing.

Printed in the United States of America, North Mankato, Minnesota
042016
092016

Cover Photo: Paul Spinelli/AP Images
Interior Photos: Paul Spinelli/AP Images, 1; AP Images, 4-5, 8-9, 16-17, 18-19, 20, 22-23, 24; Al Messerschmidt/AP Images, 6-7; Bettmann/Corbis, 10-11; Robert Klein/AP Images, 12-13; NFL Photos/AP Images, 14-15; Tony Tomsic/AP Images, 21; Kevork Djansezian/AP Images, 25; Marcio Jose Sanchez/AP Images, 26-27; Ben Margot/AP Images, 28; Bill Nichols/AP Images, 29

Editor: Patrick Donnelly
Series Designer: Nikki Farinella

Cataloging-in-Publication Data
Names: Kelley, Patrick, author.
Title: Oakland Raiders / by Patrick Kelley.
Description: Minneapolis, MN : Abdo Publishing, [2017] | Series: NFL up close |
    Includes index.
Identifiers: LCCN 2015960454 | ISBN 9781680782288 (lib. bdg.) |
    ISBN 9781680776393 (ebook)
Subjects: LCSH: Oakland Raiders (Football team)--History--Juvenile
    literature. | National Football League--Juvenile literature. | Football--Juvenile
    literature. | Professional sports--Juvenile literature. | Football teams--
    California--Juvenile literature.
Classification: DDC 796.332--dc23
LC record available at http://lccn.loc.gov/2015960454

TABLE OF CONTENTS

ALLEN'S RUN

Raiders running back Marcus Allen took a handoff from quarterback Jim Plunkett and cut to his left. Allen stopped immediately. Washington safety Ken Coffey was closing in on him. Allen turned around and ran back to his right.

Coffey reached out and brushed the back of Allen's jersey. But the Los Angeles Raiders' star running back was too fast. Coffey could not hold on. Allen split the Washington defense. Then he found another gear and raced past two more defenders.

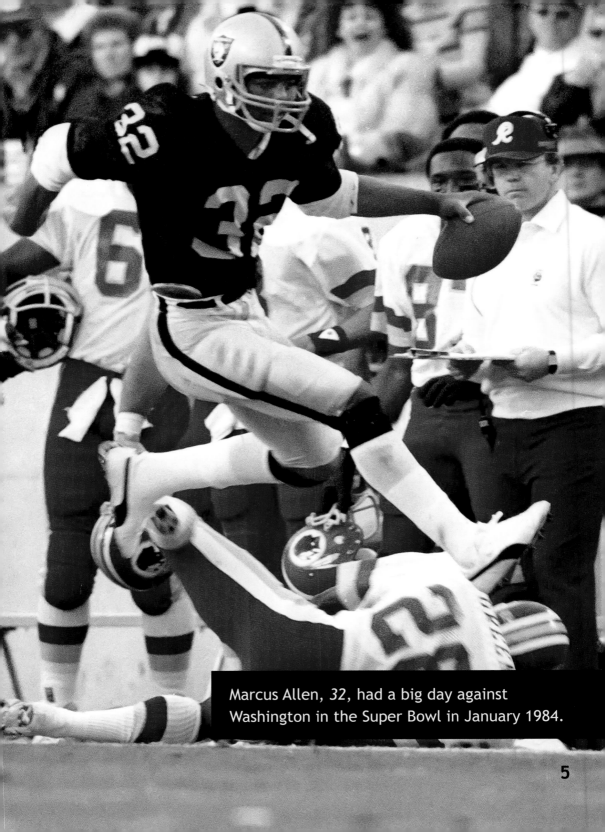

Marcus Allen, *32*, had a big day against Washington in the Super Bowl in January 1984.

FAST FACT

Marcus Allen set a Super Bowl single-game rushing record at the time. However, the record only stood for four years.

Seconds later, Allen coasted into the end zone for a Raiders touchdown. The spectacular 74-yard run was the highlight of the Raiders' 38-9 Super Bowl victory in January 1984.

Allen had a Hall of Fame career as a running back. His performance in that Super Bowl might have been his best. He ran for 191 yards and two touchdowns that day. He earned Super Bowl Most Valuable Player (MVP) honors.

Marcus Allen breaks another big run against Washington in the Super Bowl.

8

FAST FACT
Marcus Allen ran for 12,243 yards in his 16-year career. His 145 career touchdowns put him in sixth place in league history.

That game was a great one for Allen. It was also a great game for the Raiders. Allen's run helped them win the Super Bowl for the third time.

Linebacker Jack Squirek, *58*, celebrates his interception return for a touchdown in the Raiders' Super Bowl blowout of Washington.

9

In the early years, the Raiders often played
before sparse crowds such as this one at
San Francisco's Kezar Stadium.

RAIDERS ARE BORN

The American Football League (AFL) began play in 1960 as a competitor to the National Football League (NFL). The Oakland Raiders were one of the original eight teams in the AFL.

On September 11, 1960, the Raiders played their first game. The Houston Oilers beat them that day 37-22. The outcome was not that important, however. Pro football had arrived in Oakland, and the fans were excited.

In their first three seasons, the Raiders lost a lot. But in 1963, they hired Al Davis as their coach. His bold, aggressive personality had an immediate effect on the team. Davis led them to a 10-4 record in his first season.

Under Davis, the Raiders became one of the toughest teams in the NFL. On the field, the team was filled with rough, hard-nosed players. Many were outcasts from other teams. They found a home together in Oakland. Raiders fans embraced the black jerseys and pirate flags that often flew in the crowd. Many began dressing up and painting their faces when attending games.

Al Davis became the Raiders' primary owner in 1972. When he died in 2011, his son, Mark, became the owner.

Al Davis, *left*, helped turn the Raiders into a winning team quickly.

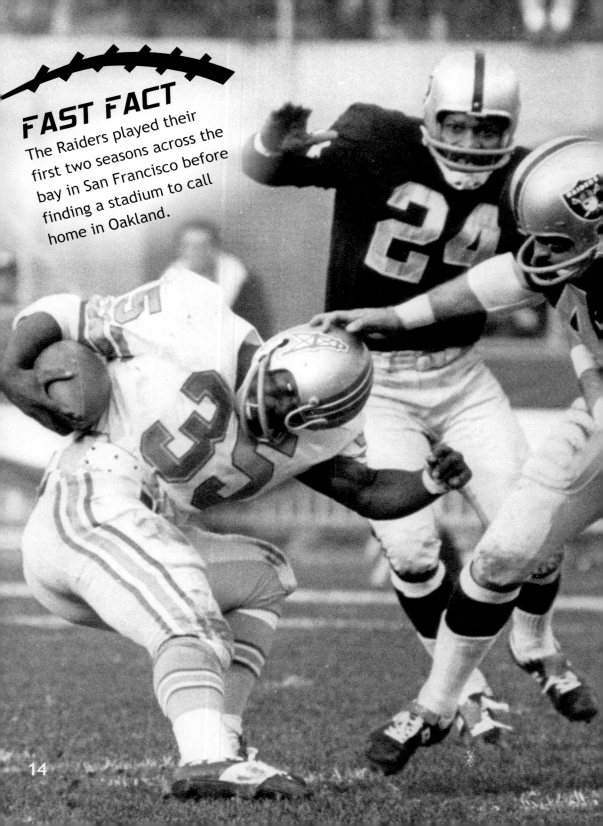

ONE OF THE BEST

Al Davis taught the Raiders to win. In 1967, the team reached a new level. That season, the Raiders went 13-1 during the regular season. Then they dominated the Houston Oilers 40-7 in the AFL Championship Game.

Two weeks later, the Raiders went to the second Super Bowl. They met the NFL champion Green Bay Packers. The Packers won the game 33-14, but that was the first of many great seasons for the Raiders.

The Raiders had their way with the Houston Oilers in the 1967 AFL Championship Game.

Daryle Lamonica was the Raiders' starting quarterback from 1967 to 1972. Fans called him "The Mad Bomber" because he liked to throw long passes. Lamonica led the Raiders to five playoff appearances in six seasons.

During the final three seasons of the AFL, from 1967 to 1969, the Raiders had a remarkable 37-4-1 record in the regular season. In 1970, the AFL merged with the NFL. The Raiders were one of 10 teams that joined the NFL that season.

Daryle Lamonica sets up to launch another long bomb against the Houston Oilers in 1969.

17

FAST FACT
From 1967 to 1977, the Raiders played in the league or conference championship game nine times.

EXCELLENCE

The Raiders had some fun with Daryle Lamonica at quarterback. But their fortunes changed after Ken Stabler became quarterback in 1973. The left-hander from the University of Alabama was called "The Snake" because he was hard to catch, and he could strike from anywhere. With Stabler at quarterback and John Madden as coach, the Raiders became one of the NFL's most feared teams.

Ken Stabler helped lead the Raiders to the top of the NFL in 1976.

In 1976, Stabler and Madden led the Raiders back to the Super Bowl. They were 13-1 in the regular season. However, their great season almost ended in the first round of the playoffs. They had to rally from 11 points down in the fourth quarter to beat the New England Patriots 24-21. That was their toughest test. They cruised past the Pittsburgh Steelers and Minnesota Vikings to win their first Super Bowl.

John Madden, *left*, and owner Al Davis admire the Super Bowl trophy after the Raiders beat the Minnesota Vikings in January 1977.

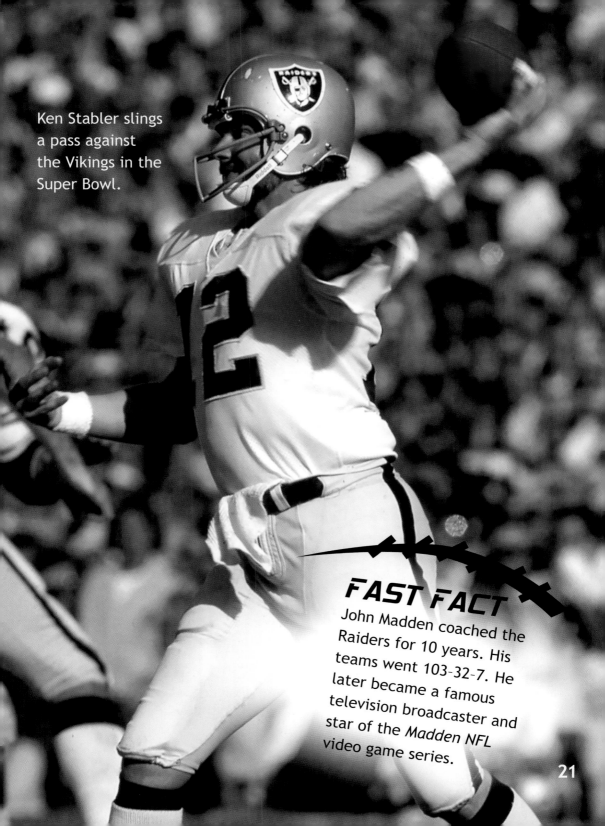

Ken Stabler slings a pass against the Vikings in the Super Bowl.

FAST FACT

John Madden coached the Raiders for 10 years. His teams went 103-32-7. He later became a famous television broadcaster and star of the *Madden NFL* video game series.

21

Tom Flores took over as coach when Madden resigned in 1979. The next year, Jim Plunkett replaced Stabler at quarterback. The new Raiders helped continue the team's winning tradition. Oakland went back to the Super Bowl after the 1980 season. Plunkett threw three touchdown passes as the Raiders defeated the Philadelphia Eagles 27-10.

Quarterback Jim Plunkett led the way as the Raiders won two Super Bowls in four years.

The Raiders moved to Los Angeles in 1982, and they kept winning. In 1983, Flores, Plunkett, and running back Marcus Allen took the Raiders back to the Super Bowl. This time, they rolled past Washington to win their third NFL title in eight years.

Tom Flores was the first Hispanic head coach to win a Super Bowl.

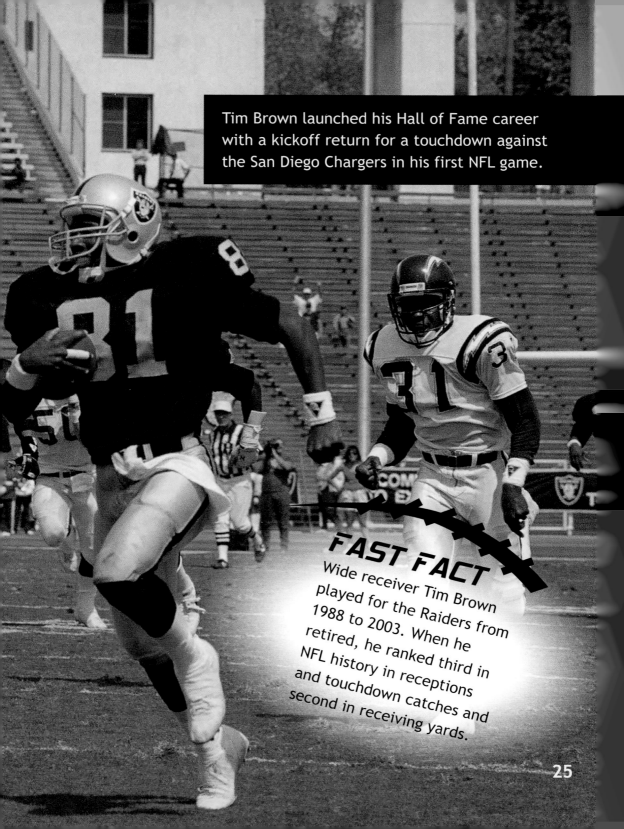

Tim Brown launched his Hall of Fame career with a kickoff return for a touchdown against the San Diego Chargers in his first NFL game.

FAST FACT

Wide receiver Tim Brown played for the Raiders from 1988 to 2003. When he retired, he ranked third in NFL history in receptions and touchdown catches and second in receiving yards.

ON THE WAY BACK

The Raiders have not won a Super Bowl since 1983, but they have had some great moments. They also changed their address again. In 1995, they moved back to Oakland.

Quarterback Rich Gannon and cornerback Charles Woodson led the Raiders into the 2000s. Gannon was the NFL's MVP in 2002. That season, he guided the Raiders back to the Super Bowl. However, the Raiders ended their great season by being blown out 48-21 by the Tampa Bay Buccaneers.

FAST FACT

Charles Woodson was the fourth pick in the 1998 NFL Draft. He spent 11 of his 18 NFL seasons with the Raiders and was known as one of the toughest cornerbacks in the league.

Charles Woodson intercepted 65 passes in his 18-year NFL career.

After 2002, the Raiders went on a skid. They did not have a winning record in any of their next 13 seasons. Better days appeared to be on the horizon, though.

Quarterback Derek Carr joined the team in 2014. The Raiders made him their top draft pick that year. He quickly became one of the NFL's best young quarterbacks. With Carr, linebacker Khalil Mack, and wide receiver Amari Cooper, the Raiders had new stars ready to lead the team back to greatness.

Khalil Mack, 52, finished second in the NFL with 15 quarterback sacks in 2015.

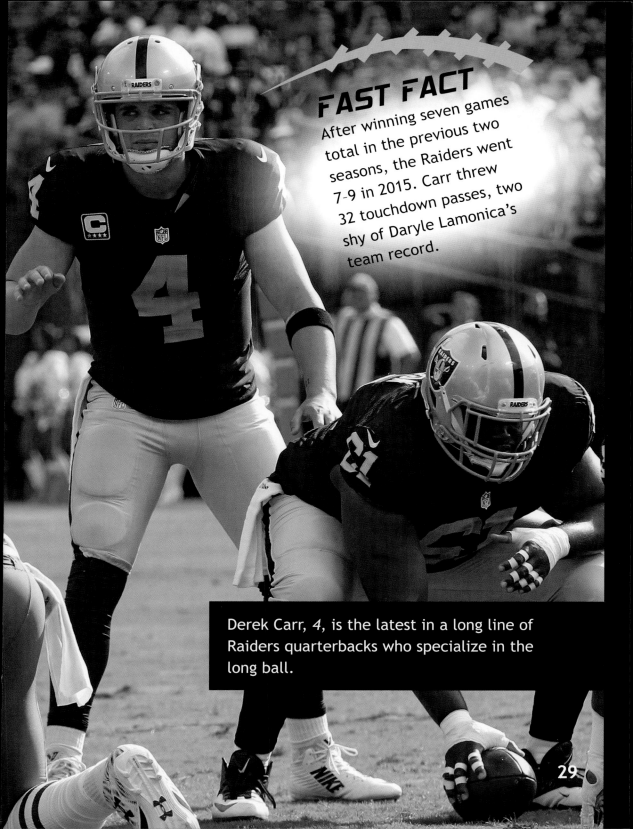

Derek Carr, 4, is the latest in a long line of Raiders quarterbacks who specialize in the long ball.

TIMELINE

1960
On September 11, the Raiders lose at home to the Houston Oilers 37-22 in their first game.

1967
The Raiders crush the Oilers 40-7 in the AFL Championship Game. Two weeks later, they lose to the Green Bay Packers in Super Bowl II.

1977
The Raiders defeat the Minnesota Vikings 32-14 in the Super Bowl.

1981
Jim Plunkett throws three touchdown passes to lead the Raiders to a 27-10 win against the Philadelphia Eagles in the Super Bowl on January 25.

1982
The Raiders move to Los Angeles and begin playing home games at the Los Angeles Coliseum.

1984
The Raiders rout Washington 38-9 in the Super Bowl on January 22.

1995
The Raiders move back to Oakland and beat the San Diego Chargers 17-7 in their first game back in the Bay Area.

2013
After spending seven years with the Green Bay Packers, Charles Woodson returns to Oakland. Woodson plays the final three years of his stellar NFL career as a Raider.

2015
In his second NFL season, Derek Carr throws 32 touchdown passes, falling two short of Daryle Lamonica's team record set in 1969.

GLOSSARY

CORNERBACK
A defensive player who covers receivers trying to catch passes.

DRAFT
The process by which leagues determine which teams can sign new players coming into the league.

HEISMAN TROPHY
The award given yearly to the best player in college football.

MERGE
When two things combine to make one.

PLAYOFFS
A set of games after the regular season that decides which team will be the champion.

RALLY
Come from behind.

RETIRE
To end one's career.

WILD CARD
A team that makes the playoffs even though it did not win its division.

INDEX

ABOUT THE AUTHOR

Patrick Kelley lives in Seattle with his wife and children. When it's not raining, he enjoys fishing, hiking, and fish tacos.